W9-CHN-169

BREAKTHROUGHS IN SCIENCE

THE EARTH

BREAKTHROUGHS IN SCIENCE

THE EARTH

CAROL J. AMATO

ILLUSTRATIONS BY STEVEN MOROS

Dedication

To Mother Earth.

A FRIEDMAN GROUP BOOK

This edition published in 1992
by SMITHMARK Publishers Inc.
112 Madison Avenue
New York, New York 10016

ISBN 0-8317-1011-X

BREAKTHROUGHS IN SCIENCE: THE EARTH
was prepared and produced by
Michael Friedman Publishing Group, Inc.
15 West 26th Street
New York, New York 10010

Editor: Dana Rosen
Art Director: Jeff Batzli
Designer: Lynne Yeamans
Layout Artist: Philip Travisano
Photography Researcher: Daniella Jo Nilva
Illustrator: Steven Moros

Typeset by Bookworks Plus
Color separations by Rainbow Graphic Arts Co.
Printed and bound in Hong Kong by Leefung-Asco Printers Ltd.

Table of Contents

INTRODUCTION

■ ■ ■ ■ ■

How did the earth form? What are volcanoes? What lies under the ocean? What are earthquakes?

These questions and others like them have aroused the curiosity of humankind since men and women first walked the planet. For thousands of years, people thought volcanoes and earthquakes and thunder and lightning were the result of the gods expressing their anger.

While modern science has answered many of these age-old questions, many other mysteries remain. We can explain, for example, the cause of thunder and lightning, but we still cannot predict with great accuracy when a volcano will erupt or when an earthquake will happen.

We do know, however, that the earth is not just a hunk of rock spinning through space, but a fragile, constantly changing organism. The planet we call home has a thin crust on the outside and a pulsing hot molten core in the middle. Its ever-changing nature spells the success or failure of the plants and animals that live on its surface. Each year, scientists uncover more and more clues revealing the miraculous workings of the only planet in the universe that we know to support life—earth.

Throughout history, and even today, discovering facts about the evolution of the earth has caused problems. The greatest conflicts have been between scientists and people whose cultural or religious beliefs and superstitions make it difficult for them to alter their views. One reason such conflicts arise is that humanity is still learning. Science no sooner answers one question than several others arise. For example, many of the scientific breakthroughs that came with the Industrial Age—such as the use of machinery or the mass production of goods—gave many people a better standard of living. But progress, along with the good, has brought some bad and has changed the earth in many harmful ways. Today we are asking ourselves questions like these: What will happen if the damage to the ozone layer, a protective layer of gases around the earth, continues? How much longer will fossil fuels last? What will happen if all the forests are destroyed? Will the average temperature of earth rise? What will the future be like for our planet?

Scientists can speculate on answers to these very important questions, but we, too, must try to help out. The earth's future is our future as well.

© E. Nagele/FPG International

The majestic Dolomite Mountains rise high above the Vallnoss Valley in Italy.

1

Early Views of the Earth's History

At left: The Egyptians believed that the earth was shaped like a rectangular box with a pillar at each corner. They thought that under the box was the river Ur-nes, where the gods sailed in boats. The Ur-nes River flowed between a mountain range that connected the pillars.

Until the time of the explorer Christopher Columbus, 500 years ago, people believed that the earth was flat. It's easy to see why people held on to this mistaken idea for such a long period of time. They could see to the horizon in all directions, and the earth certainly appeared to be flat. After all, if the earth was round, what could possibly prevent people from falling off?

The ancient Egyptians and Indians, lacking the scientific instruments that we have today, also held many mistaken beliefs about the earth. The Egyptians thought the earth was shaped like a rectangular box. They pictured this box having a flat ceiling, which was supported by a pillar at each of the four corners. The pillars were connected by a mountain range, below which there was a river they called Ur-nes. The Egyptians believed that the sun and the moon were gods who sailed in boats along this river. According to their view, Egypt was in the center of a flat earth and was surrounded by a huge ocean.

The ancient Indians' Vedic priests, who wrote down their early sacred beliefs in a collection called the *Rig Veda,* thought the earth was supported by twelve big pillars, not just four. At night, the sun passed underneath the

Above: Until the time of Christopher Columbus, most people in the Western world thought that the earth was flat.

The ancient Hindus believed that the earth stood on the backs of four very strong elephants. The elephants balanced themselves and their enormous load on the back of a tortoise. The tortoise, in turn, stood on a snake, which floated in the middle of an endless ocean.

pillars. The ancient Hindus, on the other hand, thought the earth stood on the back of four elephants. The elephants stood on a tortoise, who stood on a snake that floated in the middle of an endless ocean.

The Division of the Earth into 360 Degrees

The first people to find clues to the earth's true, round shape were the ancient Babylonians. Around 3000 B.C., they divided the earth up into 360 degrees. Each of these degrees represented the daily steps of the sun in its yearly trek across the sky. Because a circle has 360 degrees, such a discovery leads scientists and historians today to believe that the ancient Babylonians realized that the earth was shaped like a globe.

The Discoveries of the Ancient Greeks

The wise and learned ancient Greek philosophers spent much time wondering how the earth came to be. They could see that the surface of the earth was constantly changing. Several of these philosophers studied fossils and made important contributions to earth science.

❑ Aristotle's World

Aristotle (384–322 B.C.) was a famous Greek philosopher and scientist. He believed that the earth was made of four elements: earth, water, air, and fire. He thought that clouds and rain were part of the air and that the air went up to the moon. To him, the wind was the earth breathing.

Aristotle firmly believed that all forms of life fit on a scale ranging from imperfect to perfect. Creatures from the ocean, like sponges and sea anemones, were at the bottom of the scale, while humans were at the top. This view was accepted by most people until the 1600s.

While some of his ideas were wrong, Aristotle made some valuable contributions to the study of the earth. Like Pythagoras, the Greek philosopher and mathematician born in 572 B.C., Aristotle did not believe the earth was flat. He believed that the earth was sphere-shaped, and he had three pieces of evidence to support this. First, he felt that heavenly bodies were sphere-shaped when all parts tended toward the center. This was the first glimmer of the idea of gravity. Second, he pointed out that the stars appear to

Aristotle, an ancient Greek philosopher and scientist, developed many ideas that were far ahead of his time. Aristotle believed that the earth was sphere-shaped. He also proposed that scientists should study not just how the earth looks at a particular moment, but how things in nature change over time.

A total solar eclipse occurs when the moon passes in front of the sun, blocking its light. The moon is actually a fraction of the sun's size, but since it is only 239,000 miles (380,800 kilometers) from earth, while the sun is some 93,000,000 miles (148,000,000 kilometers) away, it seems to be the same size as the sun.

change in height above or below the horizon according to where the viewer stands on the earth. For instance, the brilliant southern star, Canopus, could be seen from the city of Alexandria, but not from the city of Athens. Things could only be this way if the earth was a globe. Third, he pointed to eclipses of the moon. A lunar eclipse occurs when earth, passing between the sun and the moon, casts its shadow onto the moon. Just as the earth's shadow on the moon is curved during an eclipse, so, too, must the surface of the earth be curved. In addition to Aristotle's observations, other Greeks noticed that when a ship disappeared on the horizon, the hull disappeared first, then the sails, suggesting the earth's rounded shape.

Aristotle also introduced a new idea into scientific thought—the value of observing things as they happen. He believed that the land and the sea did not remain fixed, but that the sea sometimes covered the land and sometimes receded to expose it. In addition, he believed that rivers appeared and disappeared. Because of these views, Aristotle is credited with making the first observations on the evolution of life.

❑ Eratosthenes Measures the Earth

In 230 B.C., Eratosthenes (pronounced Air-uh-*toss*-theh-neez) from the ancient city of Cyrene measured the size of the earth. Using the stadion, which was an old Greek measurement, Eratosthenes concluded that the earth's circumference was about 28,000 miles (45,000 kilometers). The real measurement is 24,902.4 miles (39,844 kilometers). This discovery is considered the first great breakthrough in earth science, because it was achieved not by guesswork but by the process of scientific reasoning.

Eratosthenes arrived at his calculation when he noticed that on June 21, the sun was directly overhead in Syene

(called Assoun, or Aswan, today), while in Alexandria, which he thought was 560 miles (900 kilometers) to the north, the sun was 7.2 degrees above the horizon. A circle has 360 degrees, so fifty 7.2-degree angles will fit in a circle. Therefore, if the earth is spherical, its circumference must be fifty times the distance between Alexandria and Syene. Eratosthenes' calculation of 28,000 miles (45,000 kilometers) was not far from the actual circumference of the earth.

Other Greek scientists also made contributions. Anaximander (610–547? B.C.) believed that the earth was suspended freely in space. The ancient Greeks also recog-

Eratosthenes stands in front of his observatory in Syene. On June 21, about 230 B.C., the sun was directly overhead Syene. Even though Eratosthenes could not actually see Alexandria, a city 560 miles (900 kilometers) to the north, he determined that the sun was 7.2 degrees above the horizon there. From this observation, Eratosthenes realized he could measure the circumference of the earth.

nized the directions of north, south, east, and west, though they believed that no other areas existed beyond the ones they knew. They called these areas "Oecumene" (pronounced Eh-kyoo-meen), meaning the "inhabited world," and drew maps of it. In 150 B.C., a Greek named Crates (pronounced Kray-teez) used Eratosthenes' maps and made a globe with the north-south-east-west lines and included the Oecumene, or known world.

Many of the Greek beliefs were accepted until the 1500s.

Beliefs on the Origin of Fossils

Fossils are remains of once-living organisms that can tell a lot about the condition of the earth before human beings were around. As mentioned earlier, several of the ancient Greek philosophers studied fossils. These men included

These 60,000,000-year-old fish fossils from the Eocene epoch were found in Wyoming. That means that part of Wyoming, if not all of it, was covered by water at that time.

© Brian Parker/Tom Stack & Associates

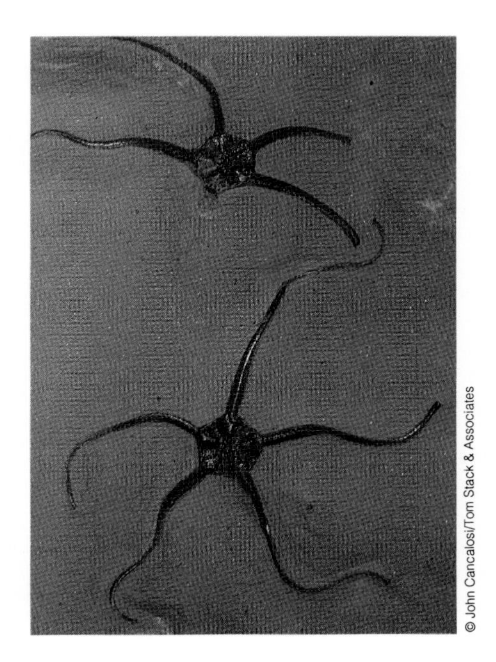

© John Cancalosi/Tom Stack & Associates

Xenophanes (Zee-*nah*-fan-eez) of Colophon (about 560–480 B.C.), Xanthus of Sardis (500? B.C.), and Herodotus of Halicarnassus (484?–425? B.C.). To them, like to most ancient peoples, fossils were anything dug up or buried. However, the ancient Greeks did believe that fossils were the remains of organisms and that the sea had once covered the area where these fossils were found.

Later on, an Arab philosopher named Avicenna (980–1037) studied many of the Greek ideas on fossils. Unfortunately, he did not believe what the Greeks said. He thought fossils were the results of nature's failure to create life out of nonliving matter. Then, a man named Albertus Magnus (1193–1280) from Cologne, Germany, claimed that fossils originated from inside the earth. Still others thought fossils were filled with germs that had fallen into crevices and developed inside rocks.

During the Dark Ages, no studies of the earth's surface occurred. Then, in the 1400s and 1500s, the Renaissance took place, and people once again became interested in science. The Italian, Spanish, and Portuguese explorers began sailing all over the world. Interest in fossils returned.

Top, left: This fossil is an ammonite. Ammonites are curved or spiral shells commonly found in Mesozoic rock. The Mesozoic era was 135 million to 225 million years ago. Top, right: These fossils are brittle stars, which are related to starfish. Even today, living brittle stars are found in all oceans, although they are most common in the tropics. There are more than 1,000 species, which vary in color. In the largest species of brittle stars, the body is about one inch (2.5 centimeters) in diameter, and the arms are about eight inches (20 centimeters) long. They eat decaying matter and microscopic organisms found on the muddy ocean bottom.

Leonardo da Vinci was extremely interested in fossils. He knew exactly what they were, but no one would listen to him. These are what some of da Vinci's sketches looked like. He wrote his notes backwards so others could not read them easily.

Leonardo da Vinci (1452–1519), a famous painter and a man far ahead of his time, was fascinated by fossils. He not only designed flying machines, including airplanes, gliders, and helicopters—which modern tests show would indeed have flown—but he began studying fossils from a scientific viewpoint.

Da Vinci knew exactly what fossils were. He wrote that they were once-living creatures that got buried in mud during floods. Unable to get out of the mud or to eat, the creatures died. As the mud hardened, the flesh rotted away, and fresh mud filled the cavity where the body had been. Drained of salt, this mud petrified, taking on the shape of the body that had been there previously.

Even though da Vinci's explanation was accurate, no one paid attention to him. Many of the views of this time were against what Aristotle had taught, and the Catholic

Church began taking a negative view of natural history as well. The Church believed instead that everyone should take the Bible literally. The Protestant churches being formed were even more fanatical about this. People began referring to fossils as "sports of nature," meaning that fossils were nature's way of playing around with different life form designs. After many conflicts and sometimes much suffering by those with unpopular ideas, the scientific nature of fossils became more obvious.

Eventually, more modern ideas about fossils started to become accepted.

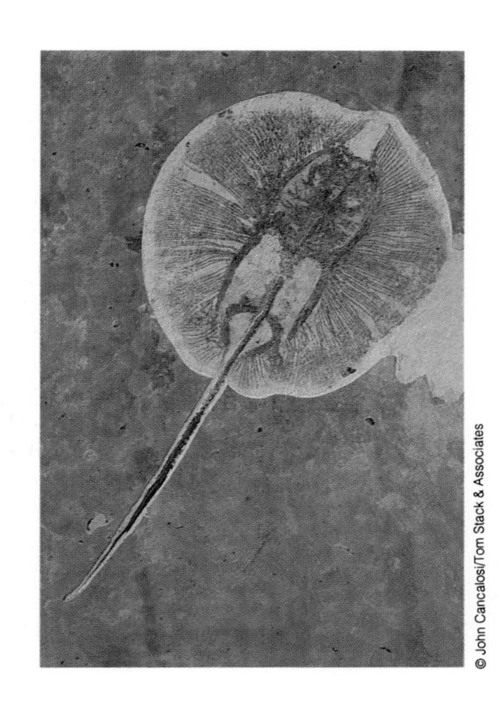

This is a fossil of a ray that dates back to the Eocene epoch, about 60 million years ago.

The Superposition of Strata

If you look at a cross section, or cutout, of the earth, you'll notice that there are different types of layers the deeper you go. These layers are called "strata." One great breakthrough in earth science occurred in the 1600s and was made by a Danish man named Niels Stensen (1638–1687), called Nicolaus Steno by the Italians. Steno developed a concept called "the superposition of strata," or, in other words, how the different layers of rock fragments, or sediment, are formed in the earth.

He devised four rules about how these layers form. First, a solid base, like rock, must exist before a layer of deposit can form. Second, the new layer of deposit must become as hard as, and therefore part of, the base before another layer can form on top of it. Third, the same strata will cover the entire earth. If it does not, it is because solid rock was higher than that strata in that location and prevented the deposit from forming. Fourth, the lower strata are older than the upper ones.

Steno's idea became one of the fundamental concepts of modern historical geology.

2

Nineteenth-Century Views of the Earth's History

THE BIRTH OF MODERN HISTORICAL GEOLOGY

Interest in the earth's strata did not end with Nicolaus Steno. In the 1700s, two men, Johann Gottlieb Lehmann of Germany and Giovanni Arduino of Italy, pioneered scientific work in this field.

In Germany's Harz Mountains, Lehmann discovered three types of mountains. The first type, the oldest ones, had structurally complex hard rocks. Horizontal mountains made up the second type, which Lehmann called *Flotegebirge* (*Floe*-teh-jeh-beer-jeh). These were composed of

The strata in these mountains are clearly visible in this photograph. Each different layer represents a different geological time period and contains different types of rocks and fossils.

© Thomas Kitchin/Tom Stack & Associates

These sandstone formations were created when the area was covered by water. The top layer is larger because the water level was below that point when it washed away the rock below. The strata are clearly visible.

deposits of sediments that were washed there by water and which contained plants and fossils. The third type of mountains were formed by accidents.

Giovanni Arduino studied the mountains in northern Italy and classified the strata into three divisions: Primary, Secondary, and Tertiary, according to the type of rocks. The Primary division included different kinds of rocks called schist, gneiss (pronounced "nice"), and rocks with quartz veins. The Secondary division was similar to Lehmann's horizontal mountains. It included limestones, marls, and clays, and these rocks all contained fossils. The Tertiary division was the youngest; this layer had limestone, sand, marl, and clay, among other things.

THE CONCEPT OF UNIVERSAL FORMATIONS

In the late 1700s, a man named Abraham Gottlob Werner (1749–1817), a professor of mineralogy at the Mining Academy of Freiberg, Germany, took a close look at Lehmann's and Arduino's work. When he was young, Werner had developed his own theory on rock strata. This included the concept of "universal formations." He claimed that when the earth first formed, it was covered entirely by water. Rocks creating the earth's crust were formed from minerals from this ocean. Werner called the rocks that formed first Primitive rocks. These included granite, gneiss, slate, and basalt, and none had fossils. The Transition class came next. This group included a form of sandstone called *graywackes* and limestones, and some fossils. On top of this were sediments of sandstone, limestone, gypsum, rock salt, coal, basalt, obsidian, and many other types of rock. He called this strata Flotz. The fourth and youngest class, the Alluvial, included sands and gravels.

© John Shaw/Tom Stack & Associates

These sandstone striations are found in Zion National Park, Utah. An ancient earthquake may have caused the rift between the two layers.

Although later evidence showed many of his theories to be incorrect, Werner was the first to talk about "geological successions"—one strata of rock laid on top of the other over time.

William Smith, the "Father of Historical Geology," produced the first geologic map of England and Wales and described the fossils found there. His work showed that scientists could use fossils to identify rock strata.

GEOLOGY BECOMES A SCIENCE

The true fundamental concept of historical geology is credited to William Smith, a surveyor who had an interest in rocks and fossils, although he had little formal education. While working on a canal project, he noticed that each strata had its own types of fossils. Furthermore, even though a certain section of strata might be physically different from another section of the same strata, the types of fossils in it remained the same. Strata, therefore, could be identified by the types of fossils in them.

Smith recorded all his findings, describing a succession of strata in central and southeastern England. He discussed their thicknesses, the types of fossils, and the rocks. In 1815, he produced a geologic map of England and Wales—

the first one of a large area—that had a list of strata from the oldest to the youngest. Smith's principles provided a chronology, or calendar, of the earth's history. His important breakthrough—that scientists could use fossils to identify rock strata—opened whole new areas of study in the earth's history. William Smith is known as the "Father of Historical Geology."

© Doug Sokell/Tom Stack & Associates

Scientists study rock strata like those pictured above to develop a geologic record of the earth's development. Each layer of rock is older than the one above it and contains its own fossils and minerals.

The Development of the Geologic Time Scale

The next great breakthrough occurred forty years later, when Adam Sedgewick (1785–1873) and Roderick Murchison (1792–1871) began studying one part of Werner's theory of rock strata, called the Transition class. This class had few fossils or complex rocks, so study was difficult.

Rocks, as we've learned, are found in layers, one on top of the other with the oldest rocks at the bottom and the youngest at the top. By measuring the age of a layer of rock and the age of its fossils, scientists began to develop a geologic time scale—a record of life on earth.

Murchison studied southern Wales and Sedgewick studied northern Wales. Murchison discovered a sequence of strata according to their fossils. In 1835, he called this sequence *Silurian,* named after the Silures, a tribe that had lived there long ago at the time when the Romans invaded Britain. He divided his Silurian system into an Upper and a Lower division.

Sedgewick discovered a series of strata in his area, too, and he called this the *Cambrian* system, from the Latin version of the Welsh name for Wales. The Cambrian system had a Lower, a Middle, and an Upper division. Eventually, the two scientists discovered that Sedgewick's Upper Cambrian had the same fossils as Murchison's Lower Silurian.

Geologic Time Chart

Eras	Systems (Rocks) or Periods (Time)	Series (Rocks) or Epochs (Time)	Approx. Ages in Millions of Years
Cenozoic	Quaternary	Holocene (Recent)	.01
		Pleistocene	2-3
	Tertiary	Pliocene	7
		Miocene	25
		Oligocene	40
		Eocene	60
		Paleocene	68-70
Mesozoic	Cretaceous		135
	Jurassic		180
	Triassic		225
Paleozoic	Permian		270
	Pennsylvanian		325
	Mississippian		350
	Devonian		400
	Silurian		440
	Ordovician		500
	Cambrian		550-600
Proterozoic			2500
Archeozoic			3800

In 1839, Sedgewick and Murchison established the *Devonian* system, which is between the Silurian and what is called the *Mississippian*. In 1840, William Smith's nephew, geologist John Phillips (1800–1874), who had worked with Smith preparing geologic maps of the English counties, expanded on his uncle's ideas. Phillips grouped the strata, using fossils from the Cambrian period to the Recent period, into three eras: the Paleozoic (ancient life), the Mesozoic (middle life), and the Cenozoic (recent life).

The Paleozoic extends from the Cambrian to the Permian systems; the Mesozoic includes the Triassic, Jurassic, and Cretaceous systems; and the Cenozoic includes Arduino's Tertiary strata, discussed earlier, and the Quaternary system.

Eventually, a uniform recording system was adopted that contained these divisions, as well as a few more. This system is still in use today.

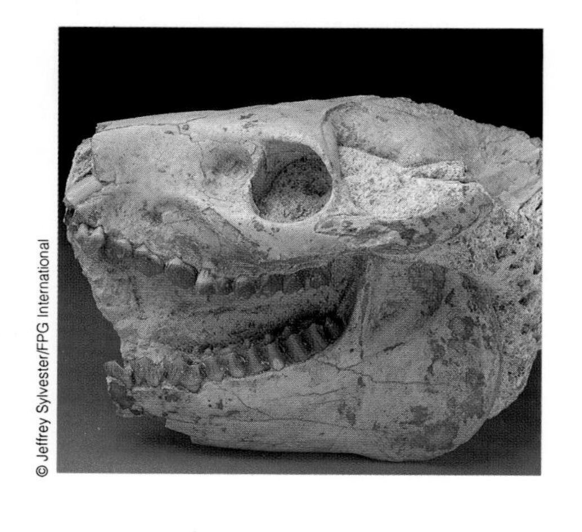

© Jeffrey Sylvester/FPG International

This fossilized skull is evidence that this animal was rapidly buried in a lake or swamp after it died. Bones and teeth preserve very well.

Fossils as a Key to Ancient Ecology

As discussed earlier, to ancient people, fossils were anything dug up or buried. To modern scientists, however, fossils are any recognizable organic structure, or an impression of such a structure, preserved from prehistoric times. Generally, only the hard parts, like shells or bones, are preserved. To become a fossil, a life form must be rapidly buried in a substance, like mud, that keeps it from being eaten or destroyed by weather. Since mud conditions are more often found in water, lakes, swamps, and on flood plains, this is where most fossils are found. Many frozen woolly mammoths from prehistoric times were found in Siberia in this century. Their skin, flesh, and internal organs are perfectly preserved.

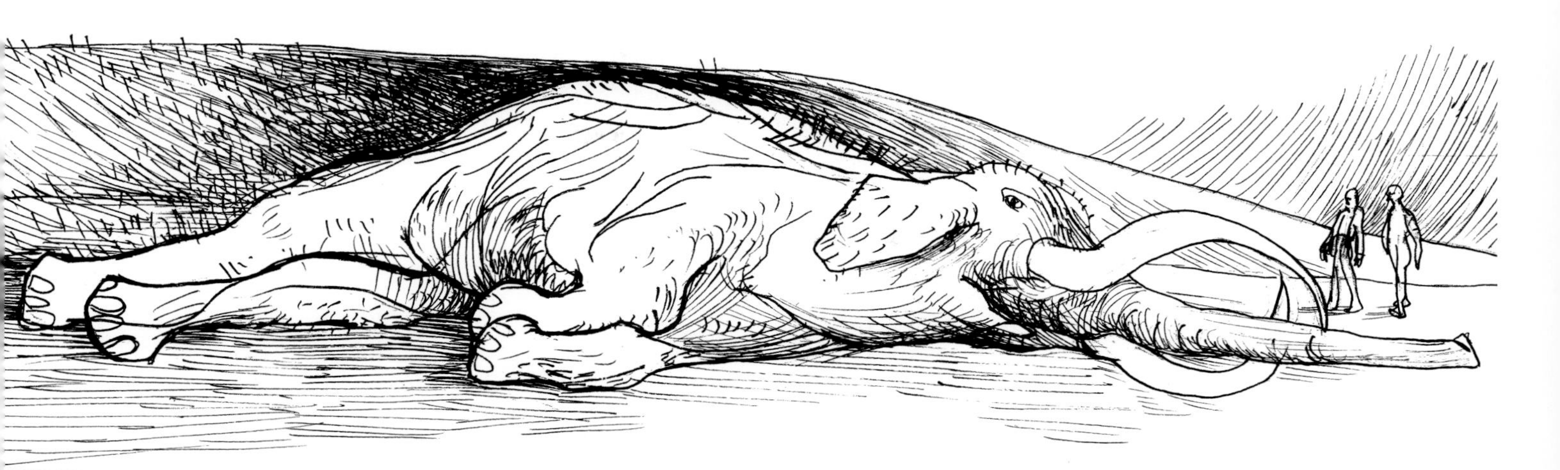

Most fossils, however, are only skeletal remains. Just as da Vinci thought, the structures became filled with mineral substances carried by ground water, which eventually petrified and took on the shape of the original body. This is called *premineralization,* and the fossil weighs more than the original organism.

Fossils are important not only because they can be used to date rock strata, but because they can tell us what kinds of plants and animals lived during the time that the strata was formed. That information provides most of our understanding of ancient environments, ancient geography, evolution, and earth chronology.

The study of ancient environments is called *paleoecology.* The conclusions drawn about the ancient environments are largely based on comparisons among fossils found in the same or a similar environment, the types of different fossil forms, and the types of rocks in which the fossils were found.

Fossils are also indicators of ancient geography, or *paleogeography.* Most plants and animals live only in certain climates. If we find fossils of sealife in the desert, for instance, we know that an ocean must once have covered that area.

Top: Scientists have discovered the remains of woolly mammoths in Siberia. In prehistoric times, these mammoths were probably buried alive in an avalanche, where they quickly froze to death. The ice kept their bodies perfectly preserved. Bottom: This is a fossil of a fish called an "ichthyosaurier."

© Jeffrey Sylvester/FPG International

A fossil can be the impression of a plant or animal preserved in the earth's crust. This fossil contains the impression of a fish. By looking at the various fossils found in a particular area, scientists can get a reasonably accurate picture of the geography and climate of that area during particular periods.

Geologists call the areas where certain plants and animals are found "zoogeographic provinces." For instance, plants and animals that evolved in hot climates will not be found in areas where it is cold, because they could not survive, and vice versa. If a fossil of a plant or animal that lived in a cold climate is found in an area that is now warm, we know that the area was cold when that animal was alive. From these ancient plant and animal fossils, geologists can make maps detailing the conditions of particular times in the earth's history.

Fossils also tell biologists about evolution, which is considered now to be a fact, not a theory. Evolution is how plants and animals change over time, and it is discussed later. The data from many different fields of science, including paleontology, anatomy, embryology, and biochemistry, all support biologists' views on evolution.

The Theory of Uniformitarianism

How old is the earth? Until the 1800s, people thought the earth was 6,000 years old, because in 1650, Archbishop James Ussher of Armagh, Ireland, claimed that the earth was created at 9 A.M. on October 23, 4004 B.C. He arrived at this number by adding up all the ages of the great men mentioned in the Bible.

In 1830, however, Sir Charles Lyell (1797–1875), an English geologist, published a book called *Principles of Geology,* in which he proposed his theory called "uniformitarianism." This theory states that the physical forces such as rain, heat, cold, moving water, and earthquakes, which change the earth today, were also at work in the past. Lyell knew that strata take a great deal of time to form. He believed that the thickness of the strata and the number of the layers indicated that the earth must be much older than originally thought. He also realized that not only was the earth old, but life had existed in various forms, some of which had become extinct, for thousands of years.

In 1864, Lyell wrote a book called *The Antiquity of Man,* and in it he supported Charles Darwin's theory of evolution.

Charles Darwin was fascinated with the diversity of the wildlife he found on the Galápagos Islands. He examined every detail of the islands, taking extensive notes and collecting specimens.

Darwin's Theory of Evolution

Until the mid-1800s, the history of the earth was thought of in purely religious terms. According to the Christian biblical story of creation, the earth was created by God in seven days, along with all the life forms on it, including humans. These life forms were created in the same form in which they exist today. Those that did not make it aboard Noah's Ark during the Great Flood became extinct.

While several people made important contributions to changing the history of the earth from a subject of religion to a subject of science and evolution, one man stands out above the rest. His name is Charles Darwin (1809–1882).

Darwin was a naturalist and a field biologist. He accepted an assignment aboard a ship called the HMS *Beagle,* which was about to begin a five-year mission to explore the world. While on this trip, Darwin noticed small differences in the beaks of some finches on an island in the Galápagos. Then he noticed that each type of finch ate different food. Some finches had powerful beaks to break up seeds, while others had short, thick beaks to eat fruit, leaves, and blossoms. Darwin concluded that the competition for different niches—environments especially suited for their occupants—led to differences in plant and animal types.

A deer's white spots help it remain unseen amid the trees. According to the theory of evolution, many deer with spots will live long enough to reproduce, while deer without spots, more easily seen by predators, will be killed in greater numbers. As a result, eventually, most deer will have white spots.

© Carl R. Sams, II/Dembinsky Photo Associates

Darwin felt that if a certain niche required certain characteristics in an animal or plant, the plants and animals having those characteristics would be the ones to survive to adulthood and reproduce, while the others would eventually die off. For example, in a wooded area, deer with white spots are harder for predators to see than all-brown deer. Because the all-brown deer are easier to see, they will probably get killed more often. That means more of the deer with white spots will survive to reproduce. Because they have white spots, and therefore the genes for white spots, chances are their offspring will have white spots, too. The ones that are born all brown will continue to be easily seen and killed, while more and more deer with white spots will grow up and reproduce. Eventually, most deer of that species will have white spots.

In Darwin's finch example, one type ate hard seeds. Perhaps at one time, that type of finch could find only hard seeds to eat. The finches with stronger beaks were able to break the hard seeds and eat them. The ones with weaker

beaks could not eat very well and so probably did not live very long. The birds with stronger beaks survived to reproduce and therefore passed on their genes for those beaks. As time went on, the weaker-beaked finches continued to die off, while the stronger-beaked ones survived to reproduce. After thousands of years, all the finches of that type had powerful beaks. This process is what Darwin called "survival of the fittest."

In 1859, Darwin published his theories in a book called *The Origin of Species.* This book caused great controversy with religious leaders, because it totally contradicted the biblical concept of how life developed. Just as it was hard for people several hundred years ago to accept that the earth was not the center of the universe, some people today find it hard to accept scientific evidence that contradicts their religious views of how life came to be. "Creationists" today still argue in favor of the religious view.

Charles Darwin studied finches in the Galápagos Islands. He noticed that birds with different types of beaks ate different kinds of foods and that their beaks seemed specially designed for the kind of food they ate.

3

Breakthroughs in Modern Geology

The Theory of Continental Drift

The earth has been in a constant state of change from the beginning of time. Various Ice Ages have come and gone. Land masses have disappeared and still others have come into existence.

Although Aristotle was the first to propose the idea of an ever-changing earth, the first person to propose the idea that the continents themselves move was a German meteorologist named Alfred Wegener. In 1912, Wegener claimed that the continents move slowly over the earth's surface. He also proposed the idea that the continents sometimes break into pieces and sometimes they collide. He called this concept *continental drift.*

The earth can be divided into various zones. The surface of the earth is called the *crust,* and it is made up of rocky material. Under the crust of the earth lies the *mantle.* The mantle is a thick shell of dense rocky matter that surrounds the planet's molten core. About 60 to 210 miles (100 to 350 kilometers) below the earth is the part of the mantle called the *asthenosphere.* Here rocks are like toffee or tar and are easily deformed. The outer 60 miles (100 kilometers) of the earth is called the *lithosphere,* where rocks are very hard and rigid. The lithosphere is made up of several plates, which Wegener believed change and move over time. He also believed that these plates move over the asthenosphere, and in the past, larger plates have broken up and smaller plates have welded together when they crashed into each other.

Scientists did not support his idea, however. They said the plates could not move without massive resistance from friction. It was not until the 1960s that Wegener's theory was proven right.

This picture shows a large crevice in the earth's crust, a crevice caused by the shifting of the earth's continents, or perhaps an earthquake.

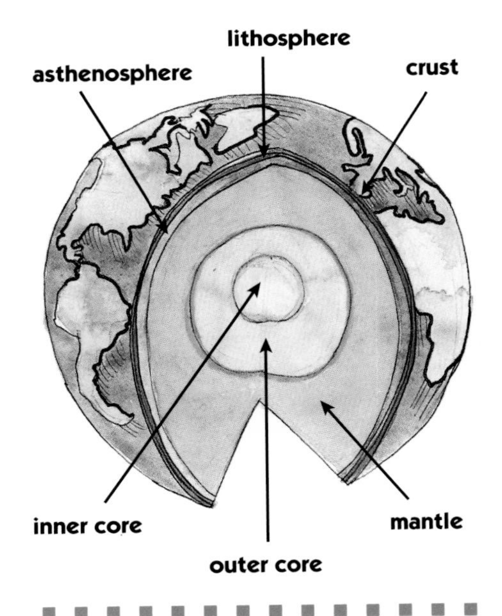

This picture shows the various layers of the earth. The inner core is made of molten material, while the lithosphere, just below the earth's crust, is hard and rigid.

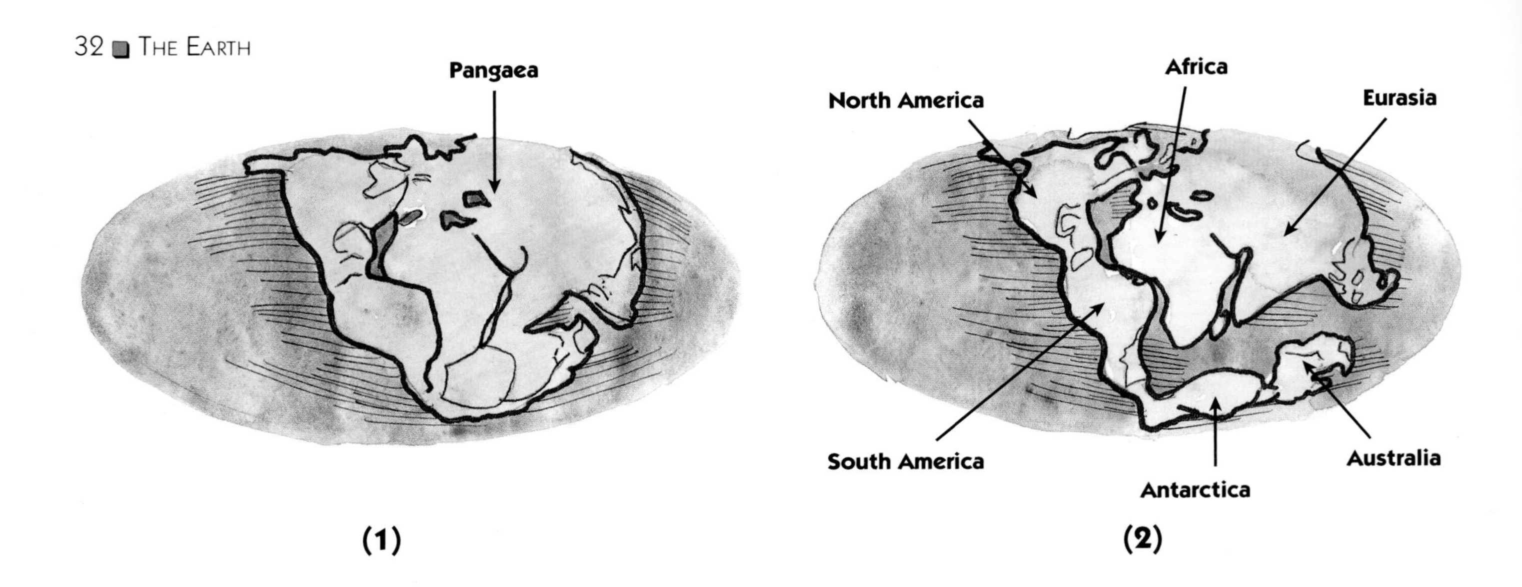

(1) Alfred Wegener proposed the idea that about 350 million years ago, the seven continents were once joined as one giant supercontinent, called "Pangaea." (2) Pangaea then began to break apart. North America drifted westward, and South America broke off from Africa. India and Antarctica split apart, and India drifted northward toward Asia. This illustration shows where the continents were placed during the Eocene epoch, about 60 million years ago. (3) By the early Quaternary period, about 3 million years ago, this was the arrangement of the continents.

Pangaea

Wegener came up with his theory of continental drift when he noticed how similar the east coasts of North and South America were to the west coasts of Europe and Africa. Doing further research, he found certain fossils from the Triassic period, which was 225 million years ago, and from earlier periods in both South America and southern Africa, but nowhere else. He also found fossils of identical trees in South America, India, and Australia. This evidence led him to believe that the earth's land masses had once been one great supercontinent. Scientists have since named this supercontinent *Pangaea* (Pan-*jee*-ah), which means "all lands." Wegener believed that during the Triassic period, the continents were in high, cold areas covered by ice. Then this supercontinent broke up, and the pieces drifted to where they are now. The pieces fit back together just like those of a jigsaw puzzle.

A geologist, Alexander du Toit (pronounced doo Twa), believed Wegener's theory about continental drift, but he was not convinced about the validity of the idea of Pangaea. He felt that there were two supercontinents, not one. The northern one, called *Laurasia* (North America, Europe, and Asia), was separated from the southern one,

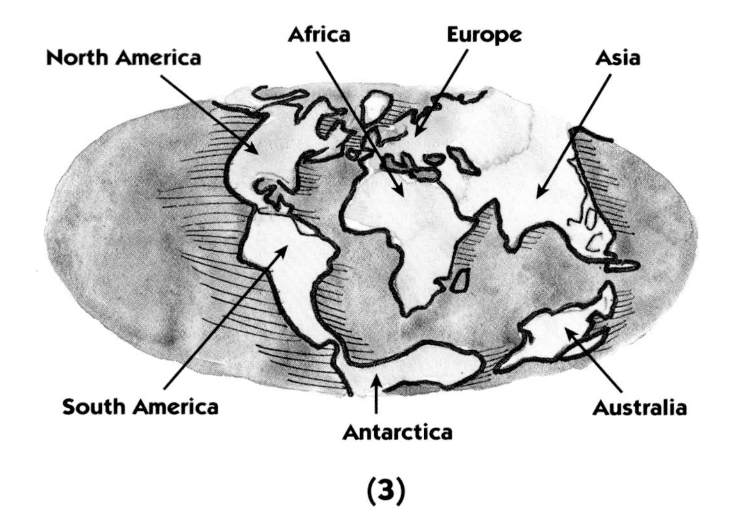

called *Gondwanaland* (Australia, Africa, South America, India, New Zealand, and Madagascar), by a narrow, now-extinct sea called Tethys. Today, Tethys' sediments are found in the Alpine-Himalayan mountain chain.

Current researchers feel that the continents during the Permian and Triassic periods were joined as Pangaea. It is likely that Pangaea started to break apart about 200 million years ago to form Laurasia and Gondwanaland.

Below: (1) Alexander du Toit believed that the seven continents started out as two supercontinents. The northern one, which he called Laurasia, contained North America, Europe, and Asia. The southern one, Gondwanaland, contained Australia, Africa, South America, India, New Zealand, and Madagascar. (2) Laurasia and Gondwanaland were separated by the Tethys Sea and eventually drifted to where they are today.

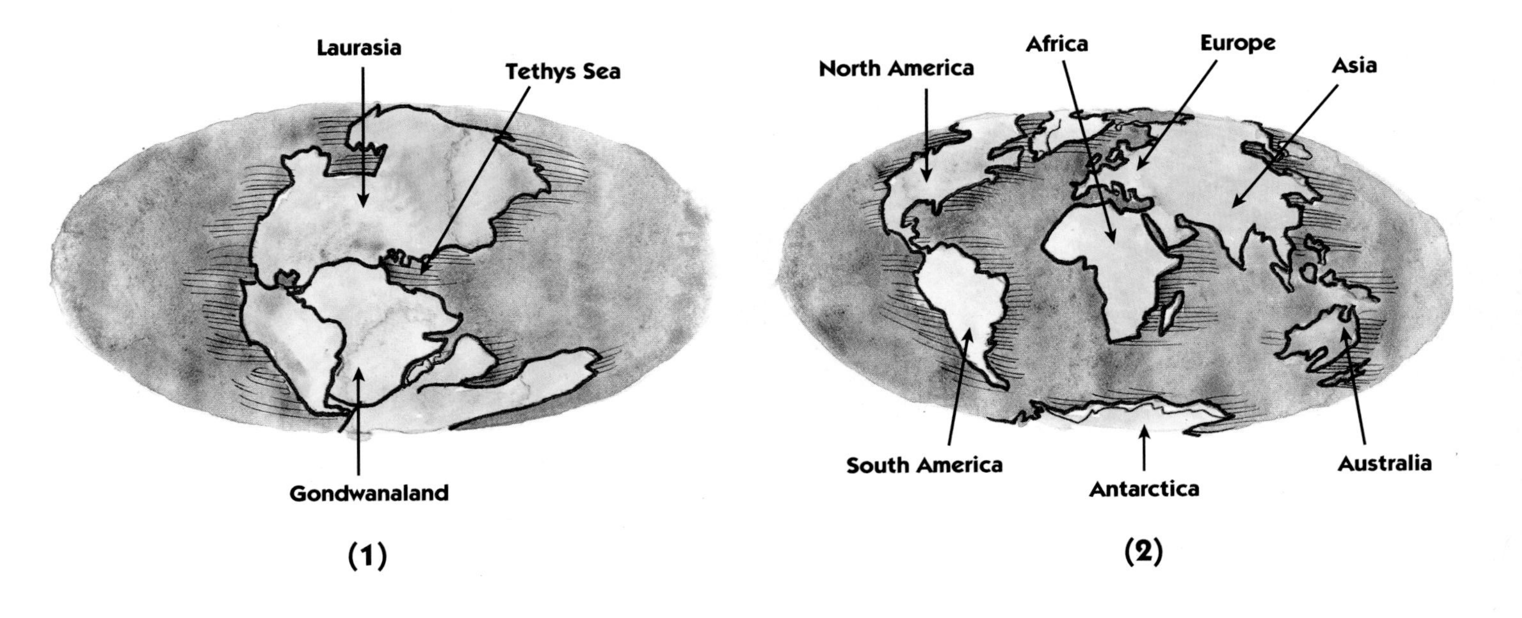

Still, during the early 1900s, many scientists were not convinced of these theories. Then, from 1955 to 1965, geophysicists made a number of discoveries. When studying old rocks, they discovered that their magnetism indicated that the North and South poles have not always been where they are now but were in different positions all over the globe at the times the different rocks were formed. This is called "apparent polar wandering." Scientists realized, however, that the poles cannot really have wandered very far from where they are located today. They also discovered that the amount of polar wandering in North America differed from that in Europe and hypothesized that the continents and rocks had moved, not the poles.

The Theory of Seafloor Spreading

Most of the ocean was unexplored until the 1950s, when scientists began to uncover many mysteries of the deep. They learned that there is a ridge in the middle of the ocean and that the sediments get thicker farther away from the ridge.

The earth is active and changing. Magma, molten rock from the earth's core, makes its way up through volcanoes on land and under the ocean and is expelled in floods of lava. Lava from this volcano in the Hawaiian islands flows into the ocean.

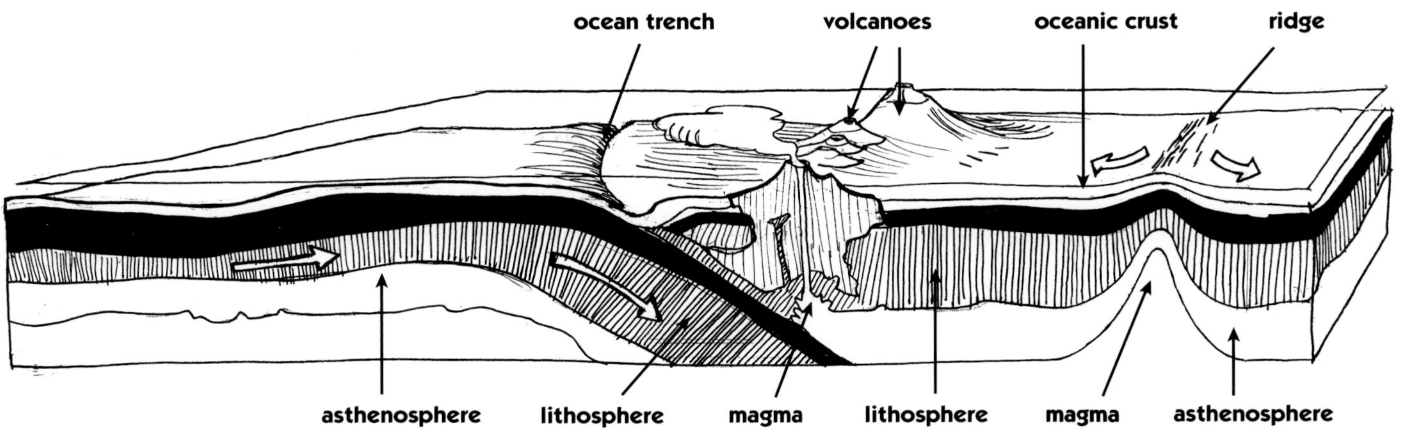

Magma rising from inside the earth forms new crust along a ridge in the ocean. Older crust is pushed aside and sinks back into the asthenosphere, causing a deep ocean trench to form. Rising magma also forms an arc of volcanoes beneath the ocean.

A Princeton University scientist named Harry Hess proposed that the seafloor continually moves sideways, away from the ridge. His idea later became known as the "theory of seafloor spreading."

The earth's crust under the ocean is called the *oceanic crust.* Hess's theory suggests that *magma* (molten rock material that forms when temperatures rise and melting occurs in the mantle or crust) from the earth's interior rises up and forms new oceanic crust along the ridge in the ocean. Hess claimed that as the new crust gets older and older, it moves farther and farther away from the ridge. Therefore, the farther away from the ridge, the older the oceanic crust.

J. Tuzo Wilson tested this theory. He claimed that if Hess were correct, volcanic islands would not only form over the source of the magma but the islands' volcanoes would be different ages. A study of the Hawaiian Islands proved Wilson right.

Another test was proposed by three geophysicists named Vine, Matthews, and Morley. They suggested that if new lava is moving away from the ridge, the oceanic crust should have a continuous record of the earth's polarity. Data gathered for antisubmarine defense research proved the three men correct.

THE THEORY OF PLATE TECTONICS

Once scientists proved that both seafloor and continents moved, they began studying these movements. This field, which is only about twenty years old, is called *plate tectonics.* The word tectonics comes from the Greek word, *tekton,* which means carpenter or builder. The discoveries scientists have made in this field have revolutionized earth sciences. It was discovered that the lithosphere not only moves, but it moves in platelike pieces that range from several hundred to thousands of miles wide. The movement of these plates causes the continents to be where they are.

Currently, there are seven large plates that move from 2.5 to 5 inches (6 to 13 centimeters) a year. They are the North American plate, the South American plate, the Eurasian plate, the African plate, the Pacific plate, the Antarctic plate, and the Indian-Australian plate. Five smaller plates also exist: the Cocos plate, the Nazca plate (both off Central America), the Phillipine plate, the Arabian plate, and the Iranian plate. These plates are made up of both land and sea. When the land part moves, the ocean floor moves in the same direction.

From this evidence, geophysicists, geologists, and paleontologists developed the "theory of plate tectonics." They claimed that the asthenosphere is very weak and fluidlike,

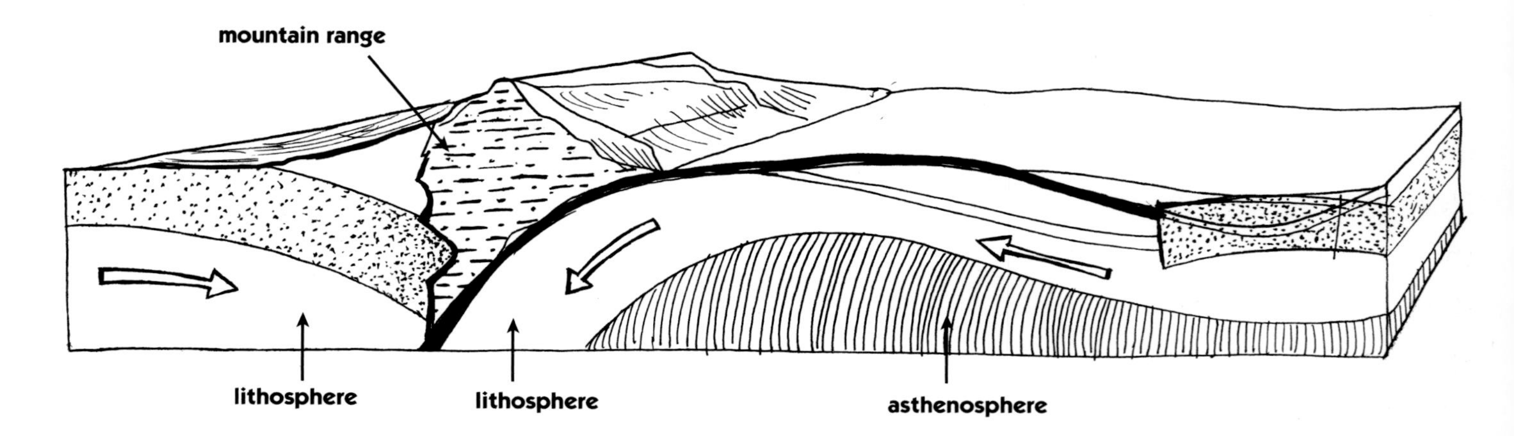

Action from the interior of the earth causes one plate of the lithosphere to collide with another. This squeezes the earth's crust upward, forming a new mountain range.

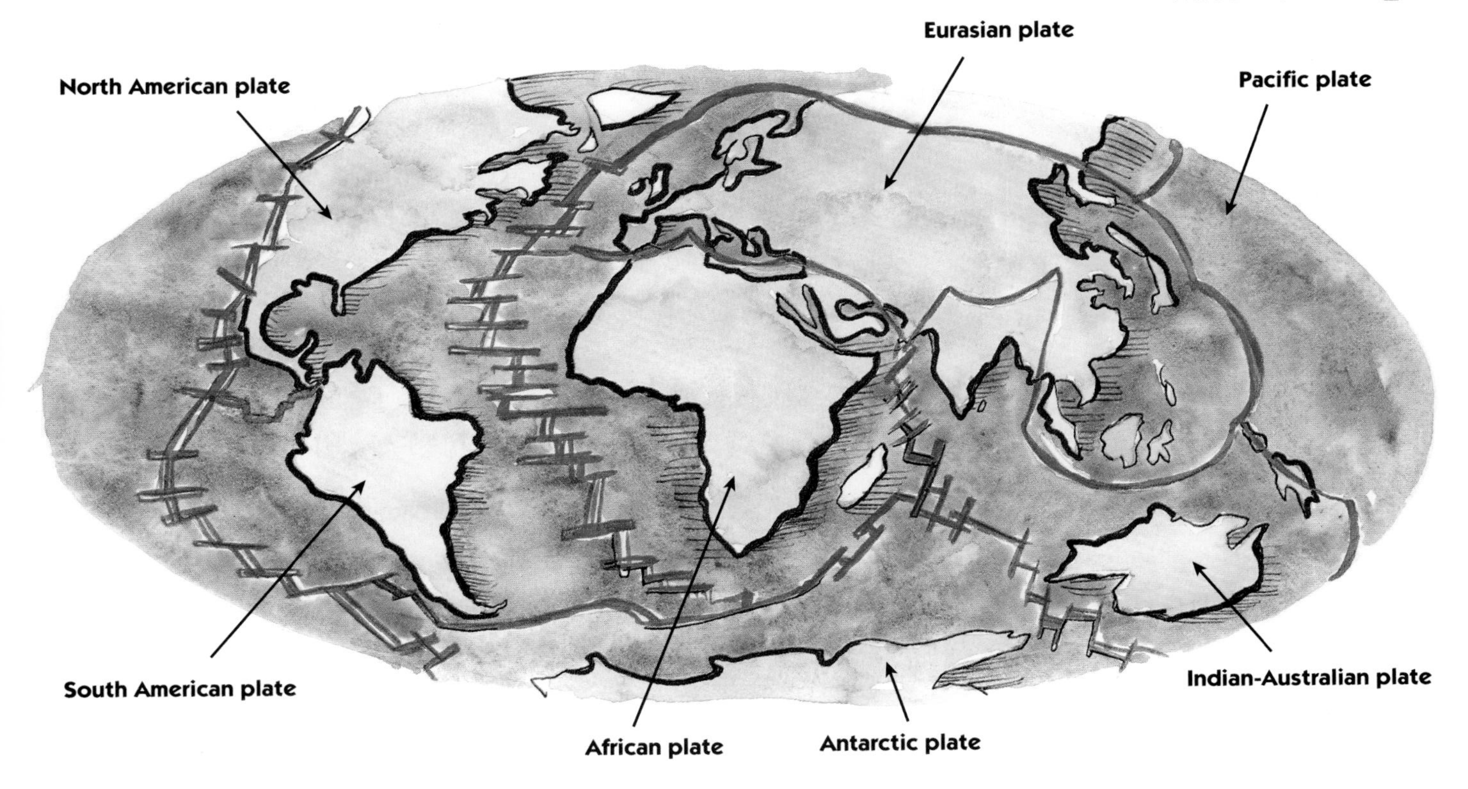

This picture shows the seven plates that make up the earth's lithosphere. As the plates shift, so does the earth's crust above them, resulting in continental drift.

while the lithosphere is very rigid. The lithosphere forms sheets that slide over the athenosphere. Since the lithosphere is thicker than the crust, as the lithosphere moves, the crust goes along for the ride. So continents do not move in and of themselves, but as parts of larger plates.

The theory of plate tectonics also explained another point. Scientists had feared that if the theory of seafloor spreading was correct, then the earth must be getting bigger and the ocean getting larger. If not, the same amount of old crust somehow had to be destroyed so the earth would stay the same size.

Scientists studying plate tectonics looked at what are called the *Benioff Zones.* The Benioff Zones are narrow areas beneath a seafloor trench where earthquakes begin. Here the old, cold lithosphere is sinking back into the asthenosphere and *mesosphere* (the area between the asthenosphere and the core/mantle boundary). The lithosphere sinks to great depths. Right now, however, scientists can only guess why the plates of the lithosphere move.

4

Breakthroughs in Geological Technology

Fusakichi Omori's seismograph, one of the first inventions to measure earthquakes, contained a column planted in bedrock through a hole in his building's foundation. A boom swung freely with the column's vibrations. At the other end of the boom was a plate with a small hole to project a bright spot onto a rotating drum covered with photographic paper.

The Development of the Seismograph

Remember the Hindus who thought the earth rested on the backs of elephants that stood on the back of a turtle who stood on a snake? These ancient people thought an earthquake was caused by the movement of these animals supporting the earth.

Today, we know differently. Scientists have learned that the earth is not a solid mass. At times, large sections of magma move, causing the rocks above to break and also causing a tremendous release of energy. This release of en-

© FPG International

This seismograph from the 1930s is much more advanced than the one Fusakichi Omori invented. Today, however, seismographs are even more sophisticated and can make much more precise recordings.

ergy causes an earthquake. The study of earthquakes is called *seismology,* and the scientist who studies them is called a *seismologist.* In the late 1800s, scientists learned that some of the energy released by an earthquake is in the form of *seismic waves,* which radiate from the *focus,* or point of origin, of the earthquake. The place on the earth directly above the focus is called the *epicenter.*

During the 1800s, a Japanese seismologist named Fusakichi Omori discovered a way to record an earthquake's seismic waves. He made an instrument that had a lever that swung with the earth's movement. This motion wiggled a light spot projected onto a rotating drum covered with photographic paper, and as the light spot moved, it made recordings on the film. Unfortunately, Omori had a hard time convincing city governments that his invention was worthwhile, but eventually they recognized the importance of his breakthrough.

Today, seismographs are very sophisticated, delicate instruments that transfer earthquake vibrations to a pen that makes marks on a moving piece of paper. The report it records is called a *seismogram*.

▫ The Development of the Richter Scale

While the creation of the seismograph allowed scientists to record the activity of an earthquake, or to see beforehand the slightest movements, it could not measure how strong the earthquake was. To fill this need, Charles F. Richter developed what he called the Richter Scale, which measures the strength of an earthquake.

Richter gave each earthquake a number, or magnitude, from one on up, according to the amount of energy released at the quake's epicenter. The magnitude is calculated from seismograph records. An earthquake with a magnitude of two is ten times greater than an earthquake with a magnitude of one. An earthquake with a magnitude of three is ten times greater than an earthquake with a

The 1989 San Francisco earthquake destroyed whole blocks of houses in the Marina district.

Earthquakes can cause damage that no one would suspect. For instance, in this picture, taken after the 1989 San Francisco earthquake, the wall is perfectly intact, yet the cars have been completely destroyed.

magnitude of two, and so on. An earthquake with a magnitude of five or six can cause major damage if it occurs in an area with buildings that are not constructed to earthquake code. An earthquake of seven or more will do damage just about anywhere. There is no upper limit to the magnitude of an earthquake, although the strongest one on record was 9.5 on the Richter Scale.

At the present time, we have no way to accurately predict when an earthquake will happen. We can estimate when an earthquake might occur by smaller foreshocks or some seismic activity in an area, but there is still no way to pinpoint when an earthquake is expected. In the future, when we can determine where and when the next earthquake will occur, we will be able to evacuate people from the area, saving lives, and control the amount of damage that the earthquake causes.

THE DISCOVERY OF CARBON 14 AND POTASSIUM ARGON DATING

In this century, a number of new methods have been devised to date rocks, fossils, and other objects. This has changed our ideas about the age of the earth and its fossils. Two of these new methods are called Carbon 14 and Potassium Argon, also called Potassium 40.

Like other radioactive materials, Carbon 14 and Potassium 40 are very unstable. Their centers, or nuclei, constantly lose particles, and this loss is called *radioactive decay.* Scientists refer to the "halflife" of atoms in radioactive material. The halflife is the time it takes for half of the atoms in a radioactive material to decay into new atoms. Carbon 14's halflife is 5,730 years, while Potassium 40's halflife is 1.3 billion years.

Let's talk about Carbon 14 first. All living organisms have large amounts of carbon. Some of this is radioactive Carbon 14. While the organism is alive, the amount of Carbon 14 it consumes as food is the same as the number lost by radioactive decay. When the organism dies, no new Carbon 14 is consumed, of course, but the atoms it already has continue to decay. When they want to date a fossil, scientists measure the amount of Carbon 14 remaining and compare it to the amount of nonradioactive carbon. By determining how much of the Carbon 14 has decayed, scientists can determine the fossil's age. Carbon 14 can be used to date any organic material, like bone, teeth, shell, charcoal, wood, and pollen. The problem is that Carbon 14 dating can be used only to date objects that existed during the last 50,000 to 70,000 years.

Potassium 40, on the other hand, can reach much further back in time. Scientists use Potassium 40 to calculate the date at which volcanic rock, like basalt or granite, cooled.

Modern dating techniques allow scientists to learn exactly how old these fossils are.

This geologist is studying rocks under a microscope.

5

The Earth as a Living Organism

All ecosystems on the earth, like the rain forests, the oceans, and the deserts, exist in a delicate balance. Humans must learn how to live in harmony with the environment instead of recklessly exploiting it for their own uses.

Many cultures throughout history have looked on our planet as Mother Earth—a place that provided nourishment for all living things. Some scientists today call nature "Gaia" and think of the earth as a living organism in which all life forms play a part to keep nature in balance. Unfortunately, many humans have not kept their part of the bargain but have set out to dominate nature and to exploit it for their own ends.

Many of the breakthroughs that scientists recently have made regarding the earth have not been ones we can be happy about. They have largely discovered how much damage humans are doing to the earth. They have realized that we cannot continue like this, or we will risk destruction of the entire planet and all the life forms on it, including humanity.

© Jeffrey Sylvester/FPG International

In Parsippany, New York, a man pickets Exxon's shareholders' meeting because the company was responsible for an oil spill that had devastating effects on the environment.

The Birth of the Ecology Movement

During the 1960s, people became aware that the earth was limited in resources and able to hold and feed only a limited number of people. They began to realize that one day we may run out of fossil fuels (oil, natural gas, and coal—products which are formed from fossils themselves) and that the population might get so large that we could not produce enough food to feed everyone. One theory claimed that as the population got larger, more and more farmland would be taken to build houses for people to live in and places for them to work instead of being used to grow food. People also became aware that our factories were polluting the air and our rivers and that polluted air and water was proving harmful to humans, other animals, and plants. These realizations led to the creation of a new science, ecology, which is the study of our environment.

Average citizens who were concerned about these problems started what has become known as the *ecology movement.* People in the ecology movement set out to educate the public about changing the course of a disastrous path before it was too late. Four of the areas they have concentrated on are overpopulation, pollution, the energy crisis, and deforestation.

Overpopulation

For quite a while, anthropologists (social scientists who study human culture and physical evolution) have known that a given area of land can house and feed only a certain number of people. This is called the land's *carrying capacity.* The more people there are, the more space is needed for houses, and that space is usually taken away from available farmland or from areas where people can hunt for food. That means less food can be grown or the animals in that hunting area move elsewhere. Eventually, the theory says, the population may increase to the point where there is no available farmland left or no animals remaining that humans can hunt.

In the past, when these problems occurred, two things could happen: The people could move to another area with more resources, or they could die.

As long ago as 1798, warnings were made about overpopulation. In that year, English economist and clergyman Thomas Malthus (1766–1834) wrote a book warning that populations tend to grow faster than the supply of goods they need. As a result, their standard of living goes down to where they can barely survive. No one paid attention to Malthus' theory, however.

Then, in 1968, a biologist from Stanford University named Paul Ehrlich wrote a book called *The Population Bomb.* Ehrlich realized that the population of the earth had increased to a point where there were no other places to move once the resources ran out. Even though people might panic and take steps to try to fix the situation, he wrote, it might be too late, because it would take fifty years to see the effects of any of the changes. In the meantime, the population would continue to grow, the resources would continue to be used up, and, eventually, nature would step in to balance the situation through famine and disease. Wars could then start and destroy the population before the corrective steps had a chance to work.

Some ecologists believe we are at such a crisis point now. What evidence do they have?

The population took *one million years* to double to the population rate present in 8000 B.C. Today, it doubles about every thirty-two years. The world's population

© Michael Hart/FPG International

This street scene in New York is typical as people go to and from work each day. Although not all areas are this crowded, overpopulation is a threat our entire planet is facing.

When towns began to industrialize, they had visions of building large plants like this one. People didn't realize that these plants would pollute the air.

reached five billion in 1986. By the year 2000, Jonas Salk, famous for developing the Salk polio vaccine, feels that the population could be as high as seven billion.

The earth is not designed to hold that many people. Many believe we are using up the world's resources fast enough to run out within twenty years.

THE ENERGY CRISIS

Before the start of the Industrial Revolution, people got as much as two-thirds of their energy from human muscle and draft animals. The main source of fuel, as it had been for over 80,000 years, was wood. With the invention of the steam engine, a new era was launched and coal mining began. Around the time of the American Civil War, coal became the primary fuel.

The fast rate of industrialization in the United States and Canada during the late nineteenth century allowed people to also use oil and natural gas, which were much cheaper and cleaner sources of energy. At the same time, Thomas Edison's electric power went into widespread use. By 1920, electric motors provided 50 percent of the power in factories. Europe, on the other hand, could not afford to make these widespread changes so quickly.

Though the United States contains only six percent of the world's population, it uses nearly one-third of the world's energy resources. Today, fossil fuels provide 95 percent of all the industrialized world's energy needs. As we mentioned, they are running out, and because they took 100 million years to form the first time, they will not exist again in the amounts available at the start of the Industrial Revolution for another *100 million years*! Current projections are that by the year 2000, fossil fuels, rather than meeting 95 percent of our energy needs, will meet only 70 percent. Even so, the United States has tripled its use of petroleum since World War II. Furthermore, use of fossil fuels, along with the dumping of toxic wastes, has caused air and water pollution and land damage. The need to develop alternate types of energy, such as harvesting power from the sun, becomes more and more pressing each year.

Early morning rush hour finds thousands of cars on the world's highways. These cars all contribute to the pollution of our environment.

Air Pollution

Our two main sources of pollution are cars and heavy industry. The car's internal combustion engine is the number one cause of pollution, sending vast amounts of poisonous lead and carbon monoxide into the air from car tailpipes. Though cars in some countries, like the United States and Canada, have smog devices to help control this, and most gas is unleaded, the problem is still severe.

Acid rain, which is rain filled with sulfuric acid and other acids from power plants, is damaging to many life forms. Some new forms of coal have less sulfur, but coal still creates large levels of nitrous oxide. Some nitrous oxides interact with sunlight and unburned traces of coal, oil, or natural gas to create smog.

Organizations have been forming throughout the industrialized world to help clean up the environment. Progress has been made, but the job is very difficult.

This autumn landscape in Glacier National Park demonstrates the incredible beauty of our natural spaces. But pollution threatens the health of the land and water across our planet.

Water Pollution

Water is polluted by oil spills from rigs, ships, pipelines, and storage tanks. Heat from power plants raises the temperature of water, and that alters the natural balance of life

in lakes, bays, estuaries, and rivers. The United States Department of the Interior estimates that 13,000 miles (20,800 kilometers) of streams and 145,000 acres (58,000 hectares) of lakes and reservoirs in the United States have been adversely affected by acid mine drainage from coal mining. Similar damage is being caused in other industrialized countries. The use of fossil fuels, especially coal, leads to solid wastes, and the runoff of this waste destroys the quality of surface water and groundwater.

Alternatives to fossil fuels are available, such as nuclear power (which has its own terrible problems with disposing of radioactive wastes), solar power, wind power, and geothermal power (steam generated from geysers, from hot water sources, and from hot rock deposits).

However, some scientists feel that we should control energy growth like we are attempting to control population growth: by ZEG (zero energy growth), meaning whatever energy we expend, we also restore.

© J.E. Stevenson/FPG International

This sewage plant in Seaford, England, dumps raw sewage directly into the ocean, thereby polluting it and destroying it as a habitat for wildlife and a place for people to enjoy.

Land Destruction

Much land has been destroyed through surface, or strip, mining and deep coal mining. Over four million acres (16,000,000 hectares) have been strip-mined for coal in the United States alone and four million more will be affected by the year 2000. Strip-mining leaves land looking gray and crater-filled like the moon and pollutes rivers and water supplies with silt and acid drainage. No recreation can take place there, and no wildlife can live there.

Another way the land is being destroyed is from underground coal mines. These mines have caused the erosion of millions of acres (hectares) of surface land, breaking roads and sewers and collapsing houses. The mine shafts under houses could be filled with material that will not settle, but the expense is so high no one has tried it.

© Dave Gleiter/FPG International

Coal strip-mining causes severe damage to the land, as you can see in this photo of a mine in LaCygne, Kansas.

Dumping of Toxic Wastes

The dumping of toxic wastes near residential areas destroys more than land. In 1978, scientists learned that toxic wastes dumped in the New York town of Love Canal in the 1940s and 1950s caused an unusual number of people there to contract cancer, produce children with birth defects, and lose otherwise healthy children to death from organ failure. An investigation, launched by housewife Lois Gibbs, revealed that the toxic wastes from the canal had seeped into the yards and drinking water of the entire neighborhood. In 1980, scientists also learned that many of the people suffered chromosome damage.

Above: To avoid contamination, these men must wear spaceman-like suits to handle toxic waste at the plant where they work. At right: Toxic waste drums sit in a pile at a dump in Oswego, New York.

DAMAGE TO THE OZONE LAYER

High up in the atmosphere is the *ozone layer.* Ozone is a blue gas that absorbs most of the sun's harmful ultraviolet radiation. Some of that radiation still reaches us, however, and this is what gives us sunburn.

In the 1980s, scientists discovered holes in the ozone layer. They learned that this damage was due to several man-made causes: the flying of supersonic jets like the *Concorde,* nuclear weapons testing, and the accumulation of chlorofluoromethane gases (chlorofluorocarbons, or CFCs) in the atmosphere. CFCs are substances used in aerosol spray cans.

We can help stop damage to the ozone layer by not using aerosol cans and by voting for measures that ban the use of ozone-damaging practices. If the ozone layer continues to disintegrate and too much ultraviolet radiation reaches the earth's surface, there could be disastrous consequences. Life as we know it could eventually cease to exist.

In early 1991, scientists learned that the ozone layer is depleting much faster than we thought. Damage to the ozone layer can cause health problems and unusual climatic changes, too.

© Charles Palek/Tom Stack & Associates

Pollution from supersonic jets like the *Concorde* and from other sources is damaging the ozone layer.

GLOBAL WARMING

Scientists have found that when fossil fuels are burned, the pollution that they release can travel long distances. For instance, scientists were confused in 1914 when they noticed that a smoglike cloud was located over Beitstad Glacier in the Arctic Ocean, a place where the air was otherwise perfectly clean. In 1984, scientists proved that this cloud was indeed pollution that had traveled from industrial cities in Europe.

This factory's smokestacks are barely visible through the haze of its polluted air. Pollution traps the sun's energy, contributing to the warming of the earth's atmosphere.

© Michael Tamborrino/FPG International

© Art Tilley/FPG International

A drought has caused this river to dry up and its bed of mud to crack.

As most smog does, it contained particles of "black carbon" from combustion engines. Because these black particles absorb the sun's energy, some scientists claim that they could lead to a substantial warming of the earth's atmosphere. This "global warming" could melt the polar ice caps and seriously alter climate patterns and surface temperatures all over the world. Farmland could become desert, and what was desert could become totally inhabitable.

THE DESTRUCTION OF THE RAIN FORESTS

Forests are ecosystems (self-sufficient environments) of living things dominated by the trees. They contain not only mature trees, but saplings and shrubs, herbs and grassy plants, earthworms, trillions of fungi, and bacteria. The trees protect these life forms. Their leaves filter sunlight, cut down on wind, and control the humidity.

Green plants are the primary source of food for all living things. Forests are very important to humans, because they help to provide most of the oxygen in our air. Plants do this through a process called *photosynthesis.* In photosynthesis, water from the soil combines with carbon dioxide in the atmosphere, and this forms a type of sugar called *hexose.* Plants give off oxygen as a waste product, and as you already know, all animals need oxygen to breathe.

Despite the fact that rain forests provide us with our oxygen, they are rapidly being destroyed at the rate of 100 acres (40 hectares) per minute. Only one-fifth of the South American rain forests are left.

There is still time, though, and always hope. If we can stop destroying the rain forests and polluting the atmosphere and waterways, we can save the planet. Such an effort, however, will take everyone's participation.

The rain forests are important because they provide our atmosphere with the oxygen we need to breathe. They also contain countless numbers of plant and animal species not found anywhere else. Some of these plants may, in fact, even hold the cures to currently untreatable diseases.

BIBLIOGRAPHY

Asimov, Isaac. *Exploring the Earth and the Cosmos.* New York: Crown Publishers, Inc., 1982.

Barney, Daniel R. *The Last Stand.* New York: Grossman's Publishers, 1974.

Briggs, Peter. *200,000,000 Years Beneath the Sea.* New York: Holt, Rinehart and Winston, 1971.

Farb, Peter. *Ecology.* New York: Life Nature Library, Time-Life Books, 1972.

Fried, John J. *Life Along the San Andreas Fault.* New York: E. P. Dutton & Co., Inc., 1973.

Gribbin, John. *Climatic Change.* Cambridge, England: Cambridge University Press, 1978.

Gribbin, John, Ed. *The Breathing Planet.* New York: Basil Blackwell and New Scientist, 1986.

Groves, Don. *The Oceans.* New York: John Wiley & Sons, Inc., 1989.

Heppenheimer, T. A. *The Coming Quake: Science and Trembling on the California Earthquake Frontier.* New York: Times Books, 1988.

Hoyt, Joseph Bixby. *Man and the Earth.* Englewood Cliffs, New Jersey: Prentice-Hall, Inc., 1967.

Imbrie, John, and Katherine Palmer Imbrie. *Ice Ages: Solving the Mystery.* Short Hills, New Jersey: Enslow Publishers, 1979.

Line, Les. *What We Save Now: An Audubon Primer of Defense.* Boston: Houghton Mifflin Company, 1973.

Maddox, John. *Beyond the Energy Crisis: A Global Perspective.* New York: McGraw-Hill Book Company, 1975.

Matthews III, William H., et al. *Investigating the Earth.* Boston: Houghton Mifflin Company, 1978.

Mayr, Ernst et al. *The Fossil Record and Evolution.* W. H. Freeman and Company, 1982.

Mitchell, John G. *Losing Ground.* San Francisco: Sierra Club Books, 1975.

Press, Frank, and Raymond Siever. *Earth.* New York: W. H. Freeman and Company, 1986.

Ross, David A. *Introduction to Oceanography.* Englewood Cliffs, New Jersey: Prentice-Hall, 1988.

Sanders, John E. *Principles of Physical Geology.* New York: John Wiley and Sons, Inc., 1981.

Skinner, Brian J., and Stephen C. Porter. *Physical Geology.* New York: John Wiley & Sons, Inc., 1987.

Spiner, Zdenek V. *Life Before Man.* New York: American Heritage Press, a Division of McGraw-Hill Book Company, 1972.

INDEX